THE LEGACY OF

THE CIVIL WAR

THE LEGACY OF
THE CIVIL WAR

BY

ROBERT PENN WARREN

Harvard University Press
Cambridge, Massachusetts
1983

This Harvard University Press paperback is published by arrangement with Random House, Inc.

Printed in the United States of America

Library of Congress Cataloging in Publication Data

Warren, Robert Penn, 1905–
    The legacy of the Civil War.

    Reprint. Originally published: New York: Random
House, 1961.
        1. United States—History—Civil War, 1861–1865—
Addresses, essays, lectures.   2. United States—History—
Civil War, 1861–1865—Influence—Addresses, essays,
lectures.   I. Title.
[E649.W27   1983]   973.7   82–21269
ISBN 0–674–52175–7 (pbk.)

To *Sidney Hook*

THE LEGACY OF
THE CIVIL WAR

THE CIVIL WAR is, for the American imagination, the great single event of our history. Without too much wrenching, it may, in fact, be said to *be* American history. Before the Civil War we had no history in the deepest and most inward sense. There was, of course, the noble vision of the Founding Fathers articulated in the Declaration and the Constitution—the dream of freedom incarnated in a more perfect union. But the Revolution did not create a nation except on paper; and too often in the following years the vision of the Founding Fathers, which men had suffered and died to validate, became merely a daydream of easy and automatic victories, a vulgar delusion of manifest destiny, a conviction of being a people divinely chosen to live on milk and honey at small expense.

The vision had not been finally submitted to the test of history. There was little awareness of the cost of having a history. The anguished scrutiny of the meaning of the vision in experience had not become a national reality. It became a reality, and we became a nation, only with the Civil War.

The Civil War is our only "felt" history—history lived in the national imagination. This is not to say that the War is always, and by all men, felt in the same way. Quite the contrary. But this fact is an index to the very complexity, depth, and fundamental significance of the event. It is an overwhelming and vital image of human, and national, experience.

MANY CLEAR AND OBJECTIVE FACTS about America are best understood by reference to the Civil War. The most obvious fact is that, for better or worse, and despite any constitutional theorizing by Governor Almond of Virginia, we are a united nation. Before the War there had been, of course, a ferocious love of the Union, but the Union sometimes seemed to exist as an idea, an ideal, rather than as a fact. There was a sense that it had to be struggled for, to be won and re-won against many kinds of enemies—not only the Burrs and Wilkinsons and Houstons and the conventioneers of Hartford, Connecticut, and the nullifiers of South Carolina, but also distance, sprawling space, apathy, selfishness, ignorance, the westward slope of the watershed beyond the Appalachians.

This unionism was, we remember, particularly ferocious in the South, as the old Jackson, the young Calhoun, and many a Whig planter, even in 1860, would testify. We can recall with what reluctance Jefferson Davis or Stonewall Jackson took the step toward disunion, and lately some historians find the corrosive of a crypto-unionism deep in many a Confederate breast less eminent than that of General Lee. When General Pickett, leading his division on the road to Gettysburg, passed a little Dutch girl defiantly waving the Federal flag, he took off his hat and bowed to her. Asked why he had saluted the flag of the enemy, he replied: "I did

not salute the enemy's flag. I saluted the heroic woman-
hood in the heart of that brave little girl, and the
glorious old banner under which I won my first
laurels." True or not, the tale, reported by LaSalle
Corbell Pickett, points to a truth. Shared experiences
of the past and shared hopes for the future could not
easily be expunged; and I myself have heard an old
man who had ridden three years with Forrest, and
never regretted that fact, say that he would have sadly
regretted the sight of this country "Balkanized."

That old unionism was, however, very different from
the kind we live with now. We do not live with an ideal,
sometimes on the defensive, of union. We live with the
overriding, overwhelming fact, a fact so technologically,
economically, and politically validated that we usually
forget to ask how fully this fact represents a true community, the spiritually significant communion which
the old romantic unionism had envisaged. In any case,
the "Union"—which we rarely refer to as a union any
more, so obvious is the fact—gives us our most signifi-

cant sense of identity, limited as that may be, and the best and most inclusive hope for our future, and that of mankind.

A second clear and objective fact is that the Civil War abolished slavery, even if it did little or nothing to abolish racism; and in so doing removed the most obvious, if perhaps not the most important, impediment to union. However we may assess the importance of slavery in the tissue of "causes" of the Civil War—in relation to secession, the mounting Southern debt to the North, economic rivalry, Southern fear of encirclement, Northern ambitions, and cultural collisions—slavery looms up mountainously and cannot be talked away. It was certainly a necessary cause, to use the old textbook phrase, and provided the occasion for all the mutual vilification, rancor, self-righteousness, pride, spite, guilt, and general exacerbation of feeling that was the natural atmosphere of the event, the climate in which the War grew. With slavery out of the way, a new feeling about union was possible.

7

Despite bumbling and vindictiveness and deprivation, many a Southerner, in one part of the soul at least, must have felt much as did the planter's wife who referred to the War as the time Mr. Lincoln set her free. As there had been crypto-unionism in the Confederate psyche, so there had been a crypto-emancipationism, or at least a deep moral, logical, and economic unease. After 1865 the terms of life were a little clearer, and one of the things clearer was the possibility of another kind of relation to the union.

THE NEW NATION came not merely from a military victory. It came from many circumstances created or intensified by the War. The War enormously stimulated technology and productivity. Actually, it catapulted America from what had been in considerable part an agrarian, handicraft society into the society of Big Technology and Big Business. "Parallel with the waste and sorrows of war," as Allan Nevins puts it, "ran a stimulation of individual initiative, a challenge to large-scale planning, and an encouragement of co-operative effort, which in combination with new agencies for developing natural resources amounted to a great release of creative energy." The old sprawling, loosely knit country disappeared into the nation of Big Organization.

It is true that historians can debate the question whether, in the long run and in the long perspective, war—even wars of that old pre-atomic age—can stimulate creativity and production. And it is true that there had been a surge of technological development in the decade or so before 1861, followed, some maintain, by an actual decline in inventiveness during the War. But the question is not how many new inventions were made but how the existing ones were used. The little device of the "jig," which, back in 1798, had enabled Eli Whitney to make firearms with interchangeable parts led now to the great mass-production factories of the Civil War—factories used not merely for firearms but for all sorts of products. The Civil War demanded the great American industrial plant, and the industrial plant changed American society.

To take one trivial fact, the ready-made clothing industry was an offshoot of the mass production of blue uniforms—and would not this standardization of fashion, after the sartorial whim, confusion, fantasy and individualism of an earlier time, have some effect on man's relation to man? But to leap from the trivial to the grand, the War prepared the way for the winning of the West. Before the War a transcontinental railroad was already being planned, and execution was being delayed primarily by debate about the route to take, a debate which in itself sprang from, and contributed something to, the intersectional acrimony. After the War, debate did not long delay action. But the War did more than remove impediment to this scheme. It released enormous energies, new drives and know-how for the sudden and massive occupation of the continent. And for the great adventure there was a new cutting edge of profit.

Not only the industrial plant but the economic context in which industry could thrive came out of the War. The Morril tariff of 1861 actually preceded the firing on Sumter, but it was the mark of Republican victory and an omen of what was to come; and no session of Congress for the next four years failed to raise the tariff. Even more importantly came the establishment of a national banking system in place of the patchwork of state banks, and the issuing of national greenbacks to rationalize the crazy currency system of the state-bank notes. The new system, plus government subsidy, honed the cutting edge of profit. "The fact is that people have the money and they are looking around to see what to do with it," said the New York magnate William E. Dodge in a speech in Baltimore in 1865. At last, he said, there was indigenous capital to "develop the natural interests of the country." And he added, enraptured: "The mind staggers as we begin to contemplate the future."

The mind staggered, and the bookkeeping in New York by the new breed of businessmen fostered by the Civil War was as potent a control for the centrifugal impulses of the South and West as ever bayonet or railroad track. The pen, if not mightier than the sword, was very effective in consolidating what the sword had won—when the pen was wielded by the bookkeeper.

Not only New York bookkeeping but Washington bookkeeping was a new force for union. The war had cost money. Hamilton's dream of a national debt to insure national stability was realized, by issuing the bonds so efficiently peddled by Jay Cooke, to a degree astronomically beyond Hamilton's rosiest expectations. For one thing, this debt meant a new tax relation of the citizen to the Federal government, including the new income tax; the citizen had a new and poignant sense of the reality of Washington. But the great hand that took could also give, and with pensions and subsidies, the iron dome of the Capitol took on a new luster in the eyes of millions of citizens.

Furthermore, the War meant that Americans saw America. The farm boy of Ohio, the trapper of Minnesota, and the pimp of the Mackerelville section of New York City saw Richmond and Mobile. They not only saw America, they saw each other, and together shot it out with some Scot of the Valley of Virginia or ducked hardware hurled by a Louisiana Jew who might be a lieutenant of artillery, CSA. By the War, not only Virginia and Louisiana were claimed for the union. Ohio and Minnesota were, in fact, claimed too—claimed so effectively that for generations the memory of the Bloody Shirt and the GAR would prompt many a Middlewestern farmer to vote almost automatically against his own interests.

THE WAR CLAIMED THE CONFEDERATE STATES for the Union, but at the same time, paradoxically, it made them more Southern. Even during the War itself, there had been great and disintegrating tensions within the Confederacy. The doctrine of States' rights did more to wreck Confederate hopes than the Iron Brigade of Minnesota and the Twentieth of Maine put together, and split the South as effectively as Sherman's March to the Sea. But once the War was over, the Confederacy became a City of the Soul, beyond the haggling of constitutional lawyers, the ambition of politicians, and the jealousy of localisms.

In defeat the Solid South was born—not only the witless automatism of fidelity to the Democratic Party but the mystique of prideful "difference," identity, and defensiveness. The citizen of that region "of the Mississippi the bank sinister, of the Ohio the bank sinister," could now think of himself as a "Southerner" in a way that would have defied the imagination of Barnwell Rhett—or of Robert E. Lee, unionist-emancipationist

Virginian. We may say that only at the moment when Lee handed Grant his sword was the Confederacy born; or to state matters another way, in the moment of death the Confederacy entered upon its immortality.

BUT LET US LEAVE THE SOUTHERNER and his War, and return to the more general effects of the War on American life. It formed, for example, the American concept of war, and since the day when Grant tried his bold maneuver in the Wilderness and Lee hit him, military thinking at Washington has focused as much on problems of supply, transport, matériel, and attrition, as it ever did on problems of slashing tactics and grand strategy.

Furthermore, on land and sea, the Civil War was a war waged under new conditions and in a new economic, technological, political and moral context. The rules in the textbooks did not help very much. The man whose mind could leap beyond the book was apt to win. It was a war fought, on both sides, with the experimental intelligence, the experimental imagination, not only in the arena of lethal contact, but in the very speculations about the nature of war. Out of the Civil War came the concept of total war, the key to Northern Victory.

A people's way of fighting reflects a people's way of thinking, and the lessons of the fighting are very apt, in a kind of dialectical progression, to modify and refine the thinking. So it may be argued that the pragmatic bias of American philosophy is not without significant relation to the encounter between the *Monitor* and the *Merrimac,* the Confederate submarine, the earthworks of Petersburg or Atlanta, the observation balloon and field telegraph, General Herman Haupt's use of the railroad at Gettysburg, the new use of mounted riflemen, Grant's systematically self-nurtured gift for problem-solving, or Sherman's theory of war.

Not that the War created pragmatism, which, in one sense, has always existed as an aspect of the human intelligence; William James called it, as a matter of fact, a new name for an old way of thinking. Some scholars have claimed that it even bears a relationship to Transcendentalism; and it developed, of course, in the new atmosphere of science in the Western world. The War did something, however, to create a climate peculiarly favorable to the formulation of this aspect of intelligence as a philosophy.

More than one historian has found in Lincoln the model of the pragmatic mind. David Donald, in "Lincoln and the Pragmatic Tradition," says that no man ever distinguished more carefully between "is" and "ought to be," and on another aspect of pragmatism quotes him: "I concluded that it was better to make a rule for the practical matter in hand than to decide a general question." And T. Harry Williams says: "One of the keys to his thinking is his statement that few things in this world are wholly good or wholly bad. Consequently the position he took on specific political issues was always a pragmatic one. His personal or inner opinions were based on principle; his public or outer opinions were tempered by empiricism."

The philosopher Sidney Hook has found in much of Lincoln's thinking and action the essential doctrines of pragmatism, for instance in the message to Congress of 1862: "The dogmas of the quiet past are inadequate to the stormy present. . . . As our case is new, we must think anew, and act anew." But in Lincoln's whole course of action, even more fully than in his words, this modern pragmatist finds the core of his philosophy: "To be principled without being fanatical, and flexible without being opportunistic, summarizes the logic and ethics of pragmatism in action."

We may turn to a man who, young, fought in the Civil War and was thrice wounded, and who, old, modified American life by his "pragmatism in action."

Justice Holmes held that the locus of law is not in the stars or in the statute book, but on the lips of the judge making the particular ruling; that "the life of law is not logic but experience," that is, "the felt necessities of the time"; that law is "predictive" of the way the force of society will act against those who would violate custom or those who would obstruct demanded change; that the document, say the Constitution (which he said is "an experiment as all life is an experiment"), cannot envisage the future contexts of applicability; that the process of seeking truth through the free collision, coil, and jar of ideas is more important than any particular "truth" found, for truth must be understood in the ever-unfolding context of needs and the *I-can't-help* of believing.

The War, we know, had made a profound impression on Holmes, nourishing his tragic sense of life and his soldierly ethic. Even granting the clear influence of Darwin and the new science, can we see Holmes'

philosophy as being a reaction from two types of absolutes, the collision of which was an essential part of the
picture of the War?

We may call these two opposing absolutes "higher
law" and "legalism."

The Abolitionist exponent of the "higher law"
claimed a corner on truth by reason of divine revelation. The man who is privy to God's will cannot long
brook argument, and when one declines the arbitrament of reason, even because one seems to have all the
reason and virtue on one's side, one is making ready
for the arbitrament of blood. So we have the saddening
spectacle of men courageously dedicated to a worthy
cause letting their nobility grow so distempered by im-
patience that sometimes it is difficult to distinguish love
of liberty from lust for blood. And we find by their
charismatic arithmetic that "if all the slaves in the
United States—men, women and helpless babes—were
to fall on the field or become the victims of vengeance
. . . if only one man survived to enjoy the freedom they

had won, the liberty of that solitary negro . . . would be cheaply purchased by the universal slaughter of his people and their oppressors."

James Redpath, the author of the above calculation, was not alone. The Reverend George B. Cheever preached that it would be "infinitely better that three hundred thousand slaveholders were abolished, struck out of existence," than that slavery should continue. The Reverend Theodore Parker welcomed the prospect of "the White Man's blood." And William Lloyd Garrison, in his characteristic style which a fellow-Abolitionist Theodore Dwight Weld described as "the vibration of serpents' tongues," proclaimed that the career of a typical Southern planter "from the cradle to the grave is one of unbridled lust, of filthy amalgamation, of swaggering braggadocio, of haughty domination, of cowardly ruffianism, of boundless dissipation, of matchless insolence, of infinite self-conceit, of unequalled oppression, of more than savage cruelty." More succinctly, he declared that "every slaveholder has forfeited his right to live." John Brown, of course, summed it all up when, with the fervor of an Old Testament prophet pronouncing on the Canaanite the blood-bath of the *cherim,* he would mutter his favorite text: "Without the shedding of blood there is no remission of sins."

One can entertain the possibility that Cornelius C. Felton, eminent Harvard Latinist and friend of Senator Charles Sumner of Massachusetts, struck the heart of the matter when he said that it seemed "as if the *love of man* meant the *hatred of men.*" What had begun as a "gnawing sense of responsibility for the ills of society at large," to take Stanley M. Elkins' formulation, "became a more and more intolerable burden of guilt" charged by all the secret confusions, frustrations, and vainglorious dreams, until, in its intolerableness, guilt was "transformed into implacable moral aggression: hatred of both the sinner and the sin." And then, to compound matters, came the longing for the apocalyptic moment, the "total solution," to purge in violence the unacknowledged, the even unrecognized, tension.

The cause for which the Abolitionists labored was just. Who can deny that, or deny that often they labored nobly? But who can fail to be disturbed and chastened by the picture of the joyful mustering of the darker forces of our nature in that just cause?

It did not matter that Theodore Weld, one of the most effective of the Abolitionists, withdrew from active propagandizing because, as he said to an admirer, he found that "he himself needed reforming," and that he "had been laboring to destroy evil in the same spirit as his antagonists." Nor did it matter that Julia Ward Howe, the author-to-be of "The Battle Hymn of the Republic," could write in 1858, after a trip to South Carolina: "Moral justice dissents from the habitual sneer, denunciation, and malediction, which have become consecrated forms of piety in speaking of the South." Nor did it matter that Lincoln could take a reasonable tone about John Brown's raid on Harpers Ferry: "Old John Brown has been executed for treason against a State. We cannot object, even though he agreed with us in thinking slavery wrong. That cannot excuse violence, bloodshed and treason. It could avail him nothing that he might think himself right."

It was certainly too late for anything to matter when, in 1862, in the *Atlantic Monthly,* Hawthorne said of Emerson's famous pronouncement on John Brown that he had never expected to "shrink so unutterably from any apothegm of a sage whose happy lips have uttered a hundred golden sentences as from that saying (perhaps falsely attributed to so honored a source) that the death of this blood-stained fanatic has 'made the Gallows as venerable as the Cross!' Nobody was ever more justly hanged." And it was far, far too late for anything to matter when James Russell Lowell, looking back, after the War, on the reformism that had flowered in that event, wrote, in his essay on Thoreau, that every form of "intellectual dyspepsia brought forth its gospel," and the reformers "stood ready at a moment's notice to reform everything but themselves." And with melancholy hindsight he added that this comic side of the period had been "the whistle and trailing fuse of the shell, but there was a very solid and serious kernel, full of the most deadly explosiveness."

Despite Theodore Weld and Julia Ward Howe and Abraham Lincoln, love of liberty and lust for blood continued to conspire to forbid much self-scrutiny or meditation on the social effects of inspired rhetoric.

The mood that prevailed did not, to say the least, cement the bonds of society. The exponent of the "higher law" was, furthermore, quite prepared to dissolve the society in which he lived, and say, with Garrison, "Accursed be the American Union." The word treason, according to the Reverend Fales H. Newhall of Roxbury, Massachusetts, had become "holy in the American language," and according to the Reverend Edwin M. Wheelock of Boston, "sacred" and "radiant." And Emerson lectured that John Brown would make the "gallows glorious like the cross." So the exponent of the "higher law" was, like Garrison, ready to burn the Constitution as a "covenant with death" and an "agreement with Hell."

But the higher-law man, in any time and place, must always be ready to burn any constitution, for he must, ultimately, deny the very concept of society. These "higher-law men" did indeed deny the very concept of society. The Transcendentalists, who had given the pattern of gospel in this matter, were men who, in a period of social change, had lost what they took to be their natural and deserved role. The country was losing leadership to the city. The banker, the lawyer, the "Lords of the loom," were taking over power from the preacher and teacher. The new business values were supplanting those of the past age. "Too distinguished a family, too gentle an education, too nice a morality," David Donald points out, "were handicaps in a bustling world of business"; and he sums up the Transcendentalists as "an elite without function, a displaced class." Henry Adams, himself an example of the elite without function, says that the Puritan in this new age "thought his thought higher and his moral standards better than those of his successors," and could not be satisfied "that utilitarian morality was good enough for him, as it was for the graceless."

Having lost access to power and importance in the world of affairs, these men repudiated all the institutions in which power is manifested—church, state, family, law, business. Men pursue and paw the individual, says Thoreau in *Walden,* "with their dirty institutions, and if they can, constrain him to belong to their desperate odd-fellow society." For all things were equally besmirched and besmirching to the ineffable and quivering purity. As Emerson says in "Man the Reformer," there is no place where the danger of besmirchment does not enter as long as one is in contact with society: "The trail of the serpent reaches into all the lucrative professions and practices of men. . . . Inextricable seem to be the twinings and tendrils of this evil, and we all involve ourselves in it the deeper by forming connections, by wives and children, by benefits and debts."

These men were reformers, but the impulse to shrink away from the besmirchment of the new society was so great that they could not bring themselves to face, practically, the most obvious abuse in that society. They railed against the values of the society, against State Street in Boston and investment banking, but to grapple with the concrete, immediate problem of poverty and exploitation would have been, for any except Orestes Brownson, too befouling, too full of the danger of involvement. So we find Garrison accusing labor leaders of trying to "inflame the minds of the working class against the more opulent." We find Samuel Gridley Howe, who had fought for liberty in Greece, had seen the inside of a German jail, and was one of the backers of John Brown, declaring that a law limiting the work day to ten hours would "emasculate" the people. And we find Emerson fretfully saying that he did not want to hear of any "obligation to put all poor men in good situations. Are they *my* poor? I tell thee, thou foolish philanthropist, that I begrudge the dollar, the dime, the cent I give to such men."

Not only would one dirty oneself by trying to reform the local system. One would have to deal practically and by piecemeal; one would, clearly, have to work out compromise solutions. But with slavery all was different. One could demand the total solution, the solution of absolute morality; one could achieve the apocalyptic *frisson*. Furthermore, since the slave grew cotton, the cotton came to the New England mills, and the mills made the new "Lords of the loom" rich, the attack on slavery had the gratifying side-effect of being, consciously or unconsciously, an attack on the new order from which the Transcendentalist had withdrawn.

He had withdrawn, and all that was left was "the infinitude of the individual"—with no "connections," with no relation to "dirty institutions," and ideally with none of the tarnishing affections of wives and children. The Transcendentalist rejoiced, as Octavius Frothingham puts it, "in the production of the 'mountainous Me' fed at the expense of life's sweetest humanities." Harold Laski, seeing even now the residual effect of this "fallacy of abstraction," describes it in *The American Democracy:* "The individual is not seen in his context as a member of a particular society at a particular time; he is seen as an individual standing outside society who can by an act of will . . . assure his own regeneration." In other words, man as a total abstraction, in the pure blinding light of total isolation, alone with the Alone, narcissism raised to the infinite power.

This is one perspective in which we can regard the Transcendentalists. In another perspective we can be grateful, not only for some of their insights and the aura of personal genius which clings about the work of some of them, but also for their role as defenders of the right to dissent, as keepers of conscience. They have most eloquently defined, we happily grant, one pole of our moral and political life. We can grant, too, that for social problems to be diagnosed, some detachment from society is necessary. Their detachment, perhaps, made their diagnosis possible.

But social problems are rarely to be solved by men totally outside of society—certainly not by men not merely outside of a particular society but outside of the very concept of society. For if all institutions are "dirty," why really bother to amend them? Destruction is simpler, purer, more logical, and certainly more exciting. Conscience without responsibility—this is truly the last infirmity of noble mind.

Nor are all social problems best solved by an abstract commitment to virtue. Before delivering his famous speech on "The Crime Against Kansas," Senator Sumner might have meditated on a passage from Aristotle's *Ethics,* with which, in his great learning, he was certainly familiar: "In discussions on subjects of moral action, universal statements are apt to be too vague, but particular ones are more consistent with truth; for actions are conversant with particulars; and it is necessary that the statements should agree with these." Or as

Lincoln said: "I concluded that it was better to make a rule for the practical matter in hand . . . than to decide a general question." But to Sumner, the angry Platonist, too many "particulars" about the situation in Kansas, or too much concern for "the practical matter," might embarrass Truth; and might lower the rhetorical temperature.

Ethics should be, indeed, the measure of politics, but there is an ethic which is somewhat different from that of individual absolutism—an ethic that demands scrutiny of motive, context, and consequences, particularly the consequences to others. This kind of ethic, laborious, fumbling, running the risk of degenerating into expediency, finds its apotheosis in Lincoln—whom Wendell Phillips felt impelled to call "the slave-hound of Illinois."

The other kind of ethic, that of personal absolutism, gives us the heroic, charged images that our hearts and imaginations strenuously demand—for instance, that of the Abolitionist Elijah Lovejoy rushing out from the warehouse in Alton, Illinois, to meet his death at the hands of the lynch mob. It even gives us the image of John Brown, abstracted from his life and from history, standing on the scaffold and drawing a pin from the lapel of his coat and offering it to the executioner to use in adjusting the hood. Such images survive everything— logic, criticism, even fact if fact stands in the way. They generate their own values. For men need symbols for their aspirations.

To return to the immediate, practical effects of higher-law-ism, the conviction, proclaimed by Wendell Phillips, that "one with God is always a majority," does not lend encouragement to the ordinary democratic process. With every man his own majority as well as his own law, there is, in the logical end, only anarchy, and anarchy of a peculiarly tedious and bloodthirsty sort, for every drop is to be spilled in God's name and by his explicit directive.

The Southern constitutionalists and philosophical defenders of slavery did not deny the concept of society.

But the version of society which these egregious logicians deduced so logically from their premises denied, instead, the very concept of life. It denied life in its defense, anachronistic and inhuman, of bondage. It denied life also, and in a sense more viciously, in its refusal to allow, through the inductive scrutiny of fact, for change, for the working of the life process through history.

This is not to say that under the impact of experience the actual South might not have been capable of change. Men are often wiser than their philosophers, and in the desperate last season the Confederate government authorized, ironically enough, the enlisting and arming of slaves, with emancipation; and at the end of March, 1865, only a week before its fall, the populace of Richmond was heartened by a public drill of Negro troops in Capitol Square, Negro troops in new gray uniforms about to go forth and repel the invaders. But despite what practical modifications the exigencies of war forced upon the Confederacy (or the exigencies of peace and developing technology might later have forced, had the Confederacy survived), the apologists offered a philosophy of marmoreal rigidity, proper to the rigidity of that society.

After the debates in the Virginia legislature in 1831, when, from a variety of motives, the question of slavery was subjected to a searching scrutiny, public discussion was at an end. It does not matter whether the end came from panic at the Nat Turner insurrection, from resentment at the attacks of Abolitionists, or from the new profits to be had from the slave system. The sad fact was that the possibility of criticism—criticism from the inside—was over. There could be no new Jefferson, the type of critic whose mind, to take the words of Stanley Elkins, "operated under the balanced tensions created not only by a repugnance to the system but also by a commitment to it." This kind of informed and morally based self-criticism, which could aim at practical solu-

35

tions, was gone. If in the North the critic had repudiated society, in the South society repudiated the critic; and the stage was set for trouble.

It is one of the paradoxes of our history that the South, which in the years before 1861 had become a closed society suppressing all criticism, should seem to become, with the firing of the first shot, extremely open. Individual rights were allowed to a degree which was, from the military point of view, disastrous. The Southerner was a first-class fighting man but a very poor soldier, and the chief reason was that he had not, as a Confederate congressman proudly pointed out, "lost the identity of the citizen in the soldier." Further, in the jealous regard for political democracy and civil rights—freedom of speech, freedom from arbitrary arrest, and due process of law—the Confederacy persisted to the point of mania. Disloyalty, sedition, profiteering and exploitation could all take refuge behind the barricade of civil rights. Despite the most violent, and sometimes venal, attacks on the government, not one newspaper in the Confederacy was ever suppressed, or even censored. The suspension of the writ of habeas corpus was, indeed, allowed three times, but only in moments of grave crisis and only with strict limitations of time and place; and when in the last desperate months Davis, who had been extremely tender in such matters, asked for a renewal of the power, he was refused by his Congress on the ground that it might encourage a dictatorial encroachment on democratic rights.

Over against this we may remember that more than 300 newspapers were, at one time or another, suppressed in the North; that Lincoln, without any by-your-leave from Congress, acting on what he termed a "popular necessity," suspended the writ of habeas corpus; that in the North upward of 15,000 persons were arrested on the presidential warrant to be held indefinitely, under presidential order, without any shadow of due process of law.

The point here is not that Lincoln was a dictator and Davis was not. One point is clearly that Lincoln was a realist and Davis was not. But there is another point—the point that interests us here. When the South, as a minority section of the Union, was acting defensively, with acute pathological suspiciousness, the legalistic and deductive bias of mind had been developed for the justification of slavery and of a society based on slavery. But as soon as, by the act of secession, the South changed its role from that of a defensive minority in the Union to that of an independent nation, the same legalistic and deductive bias of mind was free—or felt itself free—to operate on another premise, that of the individual's rights within the newly created state.

It may be that the inner motive was not basically libertarian after all, merely an extension of the old minority psychology, with the theory of States' rights and a very untheoretical individualism now directed against Richmond rather than Washington. And certainly, behind the legal scrupulosity, there was a good deal of folk pressure against dissidence, a pressure not always mild. But whatever the motive, in the new situation and new emotional climate, the old legalistic bias of mind fulfilled itself in an apparent libertarianism so extreme and doctrinaire that even the obvious necessities of victory could not contain it. The habit of mind that had worked to precipitate the War, now worked, with equal efficacy, to lose it.

But to return to the situation before 1861, the only function then left open to intellect in the South was apologetics for the closed society, not criticism of it; and in those apologetics there was little space for the breath of life, no recognition of the need for fluidity, growth, and change which life is. The philosophy of the Southern apologists did, however, offer space in its finely wrought interstices, for the bravado, arrogance, paranoid suspiciousness, and reckless or ignorant disregard for consequences that marked the Southern "fire-eater." It offered space for the anachronistic idiocy of Preston Brooks, who, on May 22, 1856, caned Charles Sumner in the Senate chamber and spilled what has been called the first blood of the Civil War.

And a little later it offered space, too, for the folly of Governor Wise and his fellow Virginians, who, instead of committing John Brown to an asylum, where all the medical evidence, even then available to the court, clearly indicated that he should be, hanged him—and thereby proved again what is never in much need of proof, that a crazy man is a large-scale menace only in a crazy society.

IN SETTING UP THE CONTRAST between the "higher law" and legalism, I have not intended to imply that the Civil War was "caused" by the extremists on both sides. That is far too simple a notion of cause, and far too simple a description of the situation. In fact, both "higher law" and legalism were reactions to a situation already in existence. But they did aggravate the situation and they did poison thinking about it; and it is not hard to see how the revulsion from the two absolutes of "higher law" and legalism—or revelation and deduction—which had, in their unresolvable antinomy, helped to drench the country in blood, could condition, not only for Holmes but for others, the tentative, experimental, "open" approach to the life process which was given the name of pragmatism. We may go even further, and hazard that the philosophy of pragmatism represented an attempt to establish the right relation between intellect and society—the relation which had been violated by the Transcendentalist repudiation of society, and Southern society's repudiation of criticism.

But to return to the notion of pragmatism as a reaction from the disastrous absolutes of "higher law" and legalism, it is not hard to see how the revulsion from the two absolutes conditions, to this day, our attitude toward our political system.

I am not referring to the fact, already noted, of Southern Democracy and Middlewestern Republicanism as results of the War. Nor to another fact, equally a result of the War: the long tradition of the Republican

Party as the party of Eastern business (captured from the Middlewestern farmers who had founded it, just as the old Democratic Party had been captured by the Southern planters from the Jacksonian farmer-labor voter), and the tradition of the new Democratic Party as the party of protest. What I am referring to is the fact that, despite the neat balance and opposition between the traditional roles of our two parties, there is an apparent illogicality in the way the system operates.

This illogicality, which appalls most foreign observers, is a logical product of the Civil War—or rather, the Civil War deeply confirmed us in a system which had gradually developed. The logic-bit foreigner, especially from a country like France or Italy, where scrupulous logicality produces some dozens of parties and where political street-fighting goes almost as unremarked as the appearance of the street-sweeper with his broom, says that our parties do not represent the real forces operating in society. In a sense the foreigner is right; if our parties do represent fundamentally opposing forces they represent them in so muzzled and domesticated a fashion that once Election Day is over, business, no matter who wins, is resumed as usual. Good business sense, as well as innate prudery, forbids that we look upon the logicality of History in all its beauty bare.

The election in which social, sectional, moral, and philosophical forces found logical projection into the party setup was that of 1860; and when the votes were counted, business was not resumed as usual. Somewhere in their bones most Americans learned their lesson from this election. They learned that logical parties may lead logically to logical shooting, and they had had enough of that. The American feels that logicality, when not curbed and channeled by common sense, is a step toward fanaticism; it tends to sharpen controversy to some exclusive and vindictive point. Chesterton said that logic is all that is left to the insane; the American is almost prepared to go him one better and say that logic is the mark of the insane, at least of the politically insane. Illogicality, like apathy (which, according to David Reisman, has "its positive side as a safeguard against the overpoliticization of the country"), makes life possible; it guarantees continuity. From the Civil War the American emerged confirmed in his tendency to trust some undefined sense of a social compact which undergirds and overarches mere political activity.

America has been full of reformers promoting everything from bloomers and Dr. Graham's bread to Prohibition and Technocracy, and perhaps in this age of complacency we should look back on them with a new nostalgic fondness; but Americans have a more and more ambivalent attitude toward such fanaticisms, however high-minded or holy. Americans freely admit that such single-minded citizens may be noble and even socially valuable; but they also feel them somewhat inconvenient. Americans don't mind enshrining a few martyrs in textbooks or naming a few high schools after them, but they do have an instinctive distaste for being made martyrs themselves to the admirable convictions of a politician who happens to have won an election. And Americans have had reason to congratulate themselves that even in the "logical" election of 1860 the successful candidate was not a "logical" politician—even though, as a result of his illogicality, he was regarded as sadly unprincipled by the logical and high-minded segment of the electorate.

The result of all this is that now a political party is a very complicated menagerie, and logically considered, the wildebeest on the extreme left of the Democratic tent looks more like the wildebeest on the extreme left of the Republican tent than like the hypocritically drowsy lion facing him from the extreme right of his own show. But to drop our metaphor, the struggle for power conducted along logical lines is much more likely to occur in smoke-filled rooms than at the polls. The party system is a grid, a filter, a meat chopper, through which issues are processed for the consuming public. The Civil War confirmed our preference for this arrangement. We like the fog of politics, with the occasional drama of the flash of a lightning bolt that, happily, is usually nothing more than a near miss.

UNION, THE ABOLITION OF SLAVERY, the explosion of the westward expansion, Big Business and Big Technology, style in war, philosophy, and politics—we can see the effects of the Civil War in all of these things. In a sense they all add up to the creation of the world power that America is today. Between 1861 and 1865 America learned how to mobilize, equip, and deploy enormous military forces—and learned the will and confidence to do so. For most importantly, America emerged with a confirmed sense of destiny, the old sense of destiny confirmed by a new sense of military and economic competence. The Civil War was the secret school for 1917-18 and 1941-45. Neither the Kaiser nor the Führer had read the right history book of the United States.

Perhaps we ourselves shall not have read the right history book if we think we can stop here and complacently cast our accounts with the past. Every victory has a price tag; every gain entails a loss, not merely the price of effort and blood to achieve the victory but the rejection, or destruction, of values which are incommensurable with the particular victory. All victories carry with them something of the irony of the fairy story of the three wishes; and even if we willingly settle for our victory we should, if we are wise, recognize that, as William James in "Pragmatism and Religion" puts it, "something permanently drastic and bitter always remains at the bottom of the cup."

With the War the old America, with all its virtues and defects, was dead. With the War the new America, with its promise of realizing the vision inherited from the old America, was born. But it was born, too, with those problems and paradoxes which Herman Melville, during the War, could already envisage when he wrote that the wind of History "spins *against* the way it drives," and that with success, "power unanointed" may come to corrupt us,

> And the Iron Dome,
> Stronger for stress and strain
> Fling her huge shadow athwart the main;
> But the Founders' dream shall flee.

The War made us a new nation, and our problem, because of the very size and power of that new nation and the nobility of the promise which it inherits, remains that of finding in our time and in our new terms a way to recover and reinterpret the "Founders' dream." Is it possible for the individual, in the great modern industrial state, to retain some sense of responsibility? Is it possible for him to remain an individual? Is it possible, in the midst of all the forces making for standardization and anonymity, for society to avoid cultural starvation—to retain, and even develop, cultural pluralism and individual variety, and foster both social and individual integrity? Can we avoid, in its deep and more destructive manifestations, the tyranny of the majority, and at the same time keep a fruitful respect for the common will? We sense that one way, however modest, to undertake this mandatory task of our time is to contemplate the Civil War itself, that mystic cloud from which emerged our modernity.

WE ARE RIGHT TO SEE POWER, prestige, and confidence as conditioned by the Civil War. But it is a very easy step to regard the War, therefore, as a jolly piece of luck only slightly disguised, part of our divinely instituted succcess story, and to think, in some shadowy corner of the mind, of the dead at Gettysburg as a small price to pay for the development of a really satisfactory and cheap compact car with decent pick-up and road-holding capability. It is to our credit that we survived the War and tempered our national fiber in the process, but human decency and the future security of our country demand that we look at the costs. What are some of the costs?

Blood is the first cost. History is not melodrama, even if it usually reads like that. It was real blood, not tomato catsup or the pale ectoplasm of statistics, that wet the ground at Bloody Angle and darkened the waters of Bloody Pond. It modifies our complacency to look at the blurred and harrowing old photographs— the body of the dead sharpshooter in the Devil's Den at Gettysburg or the tangled mass in the Bloody Lane at Antietam.

But beyond this shock and pathos of the death of 600,000 men, men who really died and in ways they would scarcely have chosen, what has the loss of blood meant, if anything, in the development of the country? The answer is, apparently, not simple. Economists calculate the potential population increase that was cut off 95 years ago and try to convert this into dollars and cents, but they do not come up with the same answer.

Some even say that the massive immigration which more than compensated for the slaughter was in itself a product of the War, and that the War, therefore, occasioned a net gain in population and consequent productivity.

Not only men, with their debatable cash value, are expended in war; property, with its more clear-cut price tag, is destroyed. Between April, 1861, and April, 1865, millions of dollars were shot away and otherwise used up in non-productive pursuits. Now it is quite clear that during the War the North enjoyed a boom. Almost everybody had reason for pocketbook-and-belly rejoicing. Quite the contrary was, of course, true in that foreign country across the Mason and Dixon Line, and as soon as the War was concluded and had established that that foreign country couldn't be foreign after all, the barren fields, ruined cities, and collapsed economy of the South became a national liability.

Everyone agrees that the chronic poverty and social retardation of the South have, in fact, been a national liability ever since, with only such gleams as William Faulkner's prose and Al Capp's cartoons to compensate for the drain. But the experts do not agree about the relation of the Civil War to the chronic poverty and social retardation. Some see the loss of capital and the massive debt structure consequent upon the War as riveting the economy to an obsolescent crop (the crop varying from one region to another) and a semi-feudal share-cropping system. But others, in denying the deleterious effects of the War, point out that twenty years after the War the South was producing more bales of cotton than ever before, that the cities had been rebuilt, and that life had, in general, returned to its old unpromising normalcy.

Some argue that the extinction of property in slaves to the value of some $4,000,000,000, to take the figure of Charles and Mary Beard, had no significant economic effect, that the change of the status from bondage to freedom did not lower, but rather enhanced, the economic value of the Negro. Some maintain, further, that even without the War the South would have run the same course—perhaps even more disastrously, stubbornly raising, with the help of uneconomic black hands, more and more bales of the fatally stultifying cotton, and that aside from any psychological or ethical considerations, the War, by breaking up the static and throttling feudal structure of slavery, did the South an economic favor and made possible what poor progress did occur.

LET US LEAVE IN SUSPENSION such debates about the economic costs of the War and look at another kind of cost, a kind more subtle, pervasive, and continuing, a kind that conditions in a thousand ways the temper of American life today. This cost is psychological, and it is, of course, different for the winner and the loser.

To give things labels, we may say that the War gave the South the Great Alibi and gave the North the Treasury of Virtue.

By the Great Alibi the South explains, condones, and transmutes everything. By a simple reference to the "War," any Southern female could, not too long ago, put on the glass slipper and be whisked away to the ball. Any goose could dream herself (or himself) a swan—surrounded, of course, by a good many geese for contrast and devoted hand-service. Even now, any common lyncher becomes a defender of the Southern tradition, and any rabble-rouser the gallant leader of a thin gray line of heroes, his hat on saber-point to provide reference by which to hold formation in the charge. By the Great Alibi pellagra, hookworm, and illiteracy are all explained, or explained away, and mortgages are converted into badges of distinction. Laziness becomes the aesthetic sense, blood-lust rising from a matrix of boredom and resentful misery becomes a high sense of honor, and ignorance becomes divine revelation. By the Great Alibi the Southerner makes his Big Medicine. He turns defeat into victory, defects into virtues. Even more pathetically, he turns his great virtues into absurdities—sometimes vicious absurdities.

It may, indeed, be arguable that in economic matters the Southerner (like the Westerner) is entitled to some grievance, and an alibi—there was, for instance, such a thing as the unfavorable freight-rate differential. But the Southerner isn't nearly as prompt to haul out the Great Alibi for economic as for social and especially racial matters. And the most painful and costly consequences of the Great Alibi are found, of course, in connection with race. The race problem, according to the Great Alibi, is the doom defined by history—by New England slavers, New England and Middlewestern Abolitionists, cotton, climate, the Civil War, Reconstruction, Wall Street, the Jews. Everything flows into the picture.

Since the situation is given by history, the Southerner

therefore is guiltless; is, in fact, an innocent victim of a cosmic conspiracy. At the same time, the Southerner's attitude toward the situation is frozen. He may say, in double vision of self-awareness, that he wishes he could feel and act differently, but cannot. I have heard a Southerner say: "I pray to feel different, but so far I can't help it." Even if the Southerner prays to feel different, he may still feel that to change his attitude would be a treachery—to that City of the Soul which the historical Confederacy became, to blood spilled in hopeless valor, to the dead fathers, and even to the self. He is trapped in history.

As he hears his own lips parroting the sad clichés of 1850 does the Southerner sometimes wonder if the words are his own? Does he ever, for a moment, feel the desperation of being caught in some great Time-machine, like a treadmill, and doomed to an eternal effort without progress? Or feel, like Sisyphus, the doom of pushing a great stone up a hill only to have the weight, like guilt, roll back over him, over and over again? When he lifts his arm to silence protest, does he ever feel, even fleetingly, that he is lifting it against some voice deep in himself?

Does he ever realize that the events of Tuscaloosa, Little Rock, and New Orleans are nothing more than an obscene parody of the meaning of his history? It is a debasement of his history, with all that was noble, courageous, and justifying bleached out, drained away. Does the man who, in the relative safety of mob anonymity, stands howling vituperation at a little Negro girl being conducted into a school building, feel himself at one with those gaunt, barefoot, whiskery scarecrows who fought it out, breast to breast, to the death, at the Bloody Angle at Spotsylvania, in May, 1864? Can the man howling in the mob imagine General R. E. Lee, CSA, shaking hands with Orval Faubus, Governor of Arkansas?

Does that man in the mob ever wonder why his own manly and admirable resentment at coercion should be enlisted, over and over again, in situations which should, and do, embarrass the generosity and dignity of manhood, including his own? Does he ever consider the possibility that whatever degree of dignity and success a Negro achieves actually enriches, in the end, the life of the white man and enlarges his own worth as a human being?

There are, one must admit, an impressive number of objective difficulties in the race question in the South—difficulties over and beyond those attributable to Original Sin and Confederate orneriness; but the grim fact is that the Great Alibi rusts away the will to confront those difficulties, at either a practical or an ethical level. All is explained—and transmuted.

The whole process of the Great Alibi resembles the neurotic automatism. The old trauma was so great that reality even now cannot be faced. The automatic repetition short-circuits clear perception and honest thinking. North as well as South (for the North has its own mechanism for evading reality), we all seem to be doomed to reënact, in painful automatism, the errors of our common past.

THE TREASURY OF VIRTUE, which is the psychological heritage left to the North by the Civil War, may not be as comic or vicious as the Great Alibi, but it is equally unlovely. It may even be, in the end, equally corrosive of national, and personal, integrity. If the Southerner, with his Great Alibi, feels trapped by history, the Northerner, with his Treasury of Virtue, feels redeemed by history, automatically redeemed. He has in his pocket, not a Papal indulgence peddled by some wandering pardoner of the Middle Ages, but an indulgence, a plenary indulgence, for all sins past, present, and future, freely given by the hand of history.

The Northerner feels redeemed, for he, being human, tends to rewrite history to suit his own deep needs; he may not, in fact, publish this history, but it lies open on a lectern in some arcane recess of his being, ready for his devotional perusal. He knows, as everybody knows, that the War saved the Union. He knows, as everybody knows—and as Lincoln, with sardonic understatement, said—that slavery was the *sine qua non* of the War. But that *sine qua non* is not enough for the deep need for justification. Even "almost all," if the all is salted with psychological and historical realism, is not enough. The *sine qua non* has to become a secretly enshrined ikon of a boy in blue striking off, with one hand, iron shackles from a grizzle-headed Uncle Tom weeping in gratitude, and with the other passing out McGuffey's First Reader to a rolypoly pickaninny laughing in hope.

When one is happy in forgetfulness, facts get forgotten. In the happy contemplation of the Treasury of Virtue it is forgotten that the Republican platform of 1860 pledged protection to the institution of slavery where it existed, and that the Republicans were ready, in 1861, to guarantee slavery in the South, as bait for a return to the Union. It is forgotten that in July, 1861, both houses of Congress, by an almost unanimous vote, affirmed that the War was waged not to interfere with the institutions of any state but only to maintain the Union. The War, in the words of the House resolution, should cease "as soon as these objects are accomplished." It is forgotten that the Emancipation Proclamation, issued on September 23, 1862, was limited and provisional: slavery was to be abolished *only* in the seceded states and *only if* they did not return to the Union before the first of the next January. It is forgotten that the Proclamation was widely disapproved and even contributed to the serious setbacks to Republican candidates for office in the subsequent election. It is forgotten that, as Lincoln himself freely admitted, the Proclamation itself was of doubtful constitutional warrant and was forced by circumstances; that only after a bitter and prolonged struggle in Congress was the Thirteenth Amendment sent, as late as January, 1865, to the states for ratification; and that all of Lincoln's genius as a horse trader (here the deal was Federal patronage swapped for Democratic votes) was needed to get Nevada admitted to statehood, with its guaranteed support of the Amendment. It is forgotten that even *after* the Fourteenth Amendment, not only Southern states, but most Northern ones, refused to adopt Negro suffrage, and that Connecticut had formally rejected it as late as July, 1865. It is forgotten that it was not until 1870 that the Negro finally won his vote—or rather, that very different thing, the right to vote.

It is forgotten that Sherman, and not only Sherman, was violently opposed to arming Negroes against white troops. It is forgotten that, as Bell Irvin Wiley has amply documented in *The Life of Billy Yank,* racism was all too common in the liberating army. It is forgotten that only the failure of Northern volunteering overcame the powerful prejudice against accepting Negro troops, and allowed "Sambo's Right to be

Kilt"—as the title of a contemporary song had it.

It is forgotten that racism and Abolitionism might, and often did, go hand in hand. This was true even in the most instructed circles, and so one is scarcely surprised to find James T. Ayers, a clergyman and a committed Abolitionist acting as recruiting officer for Negro troops, confiding to his diary his fear that freed Negroes would push North and "soon they will be in every whole and Corner, and the Bucks will be wanting to galant our Daughters Round." It is forgotten that Lincoln, at Charlestown, Illinois, in 1858, formally affirmed: "I am not, nor ever have been, in favor of bringing about in any way the social and political equality of the white and black races." And it is forgotten that as late as 1862 he said to Negro leaders visiting the White House: "Even when you cease to be slaves, you are yet far removed from being placed on an equality with the white race. . . . It is better for us both to be separated."

It is forgotten, in fact, that history is history.

Despite all this, the War appears, according to the doctrine of the Treasury of Virtue, as a consciously undertaken crusade so full of righteousness that there is enough overplus stored in Heaven, like the deeds of the saints, to take care of all small failings and over-sights of the descendants of the crusaders, certainly unto the present generation. From the start America had had adequate baggage of self-righteousness and phariseeism, but with the Civil War came grace abounding, for the least of sinners.

The crusaders themselves, back from the wars, seemed to feel that they had finished the work of virtue. Their efforts had, indeed, been almost superhuman, but they themselves were, after all, human. "God has given us the Union, let us enjoy it," they said, in a paraphrase of the first Medici pope entering upon his pontificate. Men turned their minds outward, for external victory always seems to signify for the victor that he need spend no more effort on any merely internal struggle. Few shared the moral qualms expressed by Brooks Adams in an oration pronounced at Taunton, Massachusetts, on the great centennial of July 4, 1876. He demanded: "Can we look over the United States and honestly tell ourselves that all things are well within us?" And he answered: "We cannot conceal from ourselves that all things are not well."

Brooks Adams, with his critical, unoptimistic mind, could not conceal it from himself, but many could; and a price was paid for the self-delusion. As Kenneth Stampp, an eminent Northern historian and the author of a corrosive interpretation of slavery, puts it: "The Yankees went to war animated by the highest ideals of the nineteenth-century middle classes. . . . But what the Yankees achieved—for their generation at least— was a triumph not of middle-class ideals but of middle-class vices. The most striking products of their crusade were the shoddy aristocracy of the North and the ragged children of the South. Among the masses of Americans there were no victors, only the vanquished." And Samuel Eliot Morison has written of his own section, New England: "In the generation to come that region would no longer furnish the nation with teachers and men of letters, but with a mongrel breed of politicians, sired by abolition out of profiteering."

PERHAPS THE EMINENT HISTORIANS have overstated the case. Perhaps, as some other historians say, the gusty vigor of the heroes of the period from Grant to McKinley is a tribute to the American character; and in the great a-moral economy of history their a-moral rapacity has contributed something to our present power and glory. But the process, however much it may have contributed to our advantage, was not a pretty one. James Russell Lowell, in his "Ode" for the 1876 Centennial, looked about him and addressed his countrymen:

Show your new bleaching process, cheap and brief,

To wit; a jury chosen by the thief;

Show your State Legislatures; show your Rings,

And challenge Europe to produce such things

As high officials sitting half in sight

To share the plunder and to fix things right . . .

We find, in the North, the Gilded Age, when a father could say: "Where Vanderbilt sits is the head of the table. I shall make my son rich." We find the apotheosis of what William James called the "bitch-goddess Success," and the heirs of the "sybarites of shoddy," and Jim Fisk and all the rest, including no self-reconstruction whatsoever. And in the South we find a confused and aimless Reconstruction ending in the Big Sell-Out of 1876, with the deal to make the Republican Hayes President in return for the end of any Reconstruction whatever in the South. The Republican Party, writes L. D. Reddick in *The Journal of Negro History,* "found the Negro a highly useful in-

strument to consolidate the gains made through the
Civil War. Accordingly, he was abandoned as soon
as the so-called 'New South' acquiesced in the *fait
accompli*."

The Negro didn't get his forty acres and a mule, or
anything else except a shadowy freedom, and even such
erstwhile doughty crusaders as Carl Shurz, Charles
Francis Adams, and Thomas Wentworth Higginson,
who, besides being the staunchest of the secret backers
of John Brown, had commanded the first Negro regi-
ment in the Federal army, thought that the Negro was
best left to his own devices and the ministrations of his
late masters. In any case, could any such near-socialism
as the settlement of Negroes on expropriated lands—
even Southern land—have been really acceptable to
sound Northern business sense in that heyday of ram-
bunctious young capitalism?

But the Big Sell-Out gets forgotten—except, of course,
by Negroes. There was, apparently, enough virtue
stored up to redeem even that, for the West was won,

money poured out of the plains, hills, factories, and brokerage offices, and prosperity was clearly a reward for virtue. In fact, prosperity *was* virtue—and the equation was supported not only by the old belief that virtue is rewarded by prosperity but by the new market-mentality conviction that high price in the market (*i.e.*, prosperity) is the only criterion of worth (*i.e.*, virtue). The dollars in the bank were in themselves a Treasury of Virtue; and poverty, especially Southern poverty, became a vice to be severely reprobated.

It takes little reflection or imagination to see the effect on American life of belief in the Treasury of Virtue. For one thing, as Harold Faulkner and other historians have pointed out, the reforming impulse burned itself out in the slavery controversy and it was another generation "before the nation again turned seriously to the quest for social justice." But the effects of belief in the Treasury of Virtue are with us yet. For instance, the spiritual *rentier* in the North, living on the income of the Treasury of Virtue, casts a far more tender—or at

least morally more myopic—eye on the South Side in
Chicago or on a Harlem slum than he does on Little
Rock, Arkansas, and when possible insulates himself
from democratic hurlyburly by withdrawing into pent-
house, suburb, or private school.

From 1899, when W. E. B. Du Bois published his
Philadelphia Negro, anatomizing Northern race prejudice, up to some of the articles of Carl Rowan, Negroes
have found some grim comedy in the social effects of
the Treasury of Virtue. There is another kind of comedy, equally grim and more complex, in seeing the
unregenerate Southerner join the Negro in the good
laugh at Yankee phariseeism. But others, too, have had
a right to join in the grisly hilarity—all those spooky
tribes of immigrants, from the early Irish and German
through the Jews and Scots and Poles and Italians, to
the late-arriving Puerto Ricans.

Not only foreigners who emigrated to America, but
foreigners who stayed at home, have sometimes availed
themselves of the opportunity for sardonic mirth. From

the first, Americans had a strong tendency to think of their land as the Galahad among nations, and the Civil War, with its happy marriage of victory and virtue, has converted this tendency into an article of faith nearly as sacrosanct as the Declaration of Independence.

Most Americans are ready to echo the sentiment of Woodrow Wilson that "America is the only idealist country in the world." As Reinhold Niebuhr has put it, we live in the illusions of our national infancy, the illusions of innocence and virtue. We have not grown up enough to appreciate the difficulty of moral definition, the doubleness of experience—what he calls "the irony of history."

All this is not to say that America has not characteristically demonstrated generosity, sometimes even informed generosity, in dealing with other peoples, or has not, in the course of its history, struggled to define and realize certain worthy ideals. But moral narcissism is a peculiarly unlovely and unlovable trait. Even when the narcissist happens to possess the virtues which he devotes his time to congratulating himself upon, the observer is less apt to regard the virtues than their context of pathology. Certainly, moral narcissism is a poor basis for national policy; but we have our crusades of 1917-18 and 1941-45 and our diplomacy of righteousness, with the slogan of unconditional surrender and universal spiritual rehabilitation—for others.

Even if moral narcissism did not get us into the wars, even if we should have been in the wars, the narcissism certainly did have a great deal to do with the spirit and method by which they were conducted. And it contributed no little to the sad, embarrassing, and even perilous consequences. Furthermore, in our moments of victory it is hard for us to remember the full implications of William James' remark that "the victory to be philosophically prayed for is that of the more inclusive side—of the side which even in the hour of triumph will to some degree do justice to the ideals in which the vanquished interests lay."

In all our victories the United States has, I am confident, been the "more inclusive side." And we can look at our history and see examples of the attempt "to do justice to the ideals in which the vanquished interests lay." To take a trivial and sentimental example, we can think of the glorification by Northern publishers and public of the idyl of the Southern plantation as presented by the school of Thomas Nelson Page. To take a more serious and sophisticated example, we can think of the use Melville, Henry Adams, and Henry James made, as Vann Woodward has pointed out, of Confederate characters to serve as ironical critics of the values of the Gilded Age—Ungar in Melville's epic *Clarel*, John Carrington in Adams' novel *Democracy*, and Basil Ransom in James' *Bostonians*. But Melville, Adams, and James stood outside their age, and the age swept past them oblivious of their criticism, with little concern to do justice to anything except the demands of double-entry bookkeeping. In our subsequent victories we have, I trust, done better. But have we fully accepted the obligations of our "inclusiveness"?

Wrapped in our righteousness, we sometimes feel that our solitude is, as Henry Adams said of the righteous solitude of Charles Sumner, "glacial." We are isolated in righteousness, beleaguered by lesser breeds without the law whose heads of state incline to secret diplomacy, back-stairs agreements, imperialistic exploitation, and espionage, and in general lack the missionary spirit. Not that the foreigner himself minds too much being credited with professional savvy. He rather likes that. What he finds funny is the incorruptibly automatic gleam of righteousness in the American eye.

The man of righteousness tends to be so sure of his own motives that he does not need to inspect consequences. Therefore, says Abraham Kaplan in "American Ethics and Public Policy," "any debate on principle offers the incomparable advantage of irresponsibility." He proceeds to quote Max Weber: "There is an abysmal contrast between conduct that follows the maxim of an ethic of ultimate ends—that is, in religious terms,

'The Christian does rightly and leaves the results with the Lord'—and conduct that follows the maxim of an ethic of responsibility, in which case one has to give an account of the foreseeable results of one's action." The American, in his conviction of righteousness, may be, on some occasions, morally unassailable, but for reasons that may also make him politically irresponsible.

Righteousness is our first refuge and our strength—even when we have acted on the grounds of calculated self-interest, and have got caught red-handed, and have to admit, a couple of days later, to a great bumbling horse-apple of a lie. In such a case, the effect of the conviction of virtue is to make us lie automatically and awkwardly, with no élan of artistry and no fore-thought; and then in trying to justify the lie, lie to ourselves and transmute the lie into a kind of superior truth.

The Great Alibi and the Treasury of Virtue—they are maiming liabilities we inherit from the Civil War. But at the same time they may contribute—how un-

worthily—to the attraction the War holds for us. The
Great Alibi and the Treasury of Virtue both serve deep
needs of poor human nature; and if, without historical
realism and self-criticism, we look back on the War, we
are merely compounding the old inherited delusions
which our weakness craves. We fear, in other words, to
lose the comforting automatism of the Great Alibi or
the Treasury of Virtue, for if we lose them we may, at
last, find ourselves nakedly alone with the problems of
our time and with ourselves. Where would we find our
next alibi and our next assurance of virtue?

DESPITE ALL THE COSTS, however, most Americans are
prepared to see the Civil War as a fountainhead of
our power and prestige among the nations. They are
right; and even the most disgruntled Southerner, no
matter how much he may damn the Yankee and his
works, loves as well as the next man to bask in the

beams of power and prestige. But is it our delight in power and prestige that gives the War its grip on the American imagination? No, and it is not even the fact that the effects of the War, for better and worse, permeate American life and culture—for we are so accustomed to breath that we are unaware of the air we breathe. It is not even the comfort we get from the Great Alibi and the Treasury of Virtue.

No one thing accounts for the appeal of the Civil War, certainly not the simple piety of family or region, which once was so important in the matter. We see the marks of that old piety in the sad little monument on the village green in Vermont or in the square in East Texas. But for a long time America has been on the move, and local pieties wear thin. Family pieties and family ties, they thin, too, with time. Relatively few Americans now alive once sat by the grandfather's knee to hear how the men of Pickett and Pettigrew held formation up the ridge at Gettysburg, or how dogwood bloomed white in the dark woods of Shiloh.

It is not merely that few men now alive can, chrono-
logically, have known the grandfather who had been
in the War; the grandfather, or great-grandfather, of
a high proportion of our population was not even in
this country when the War was being fought. Not that
this disqualifies the grandson from experiencing to the
full the imaginative appeal of the Civil War. To experience this appeal may be, in fact, the very ritual of
being American. A man with an Italian name may don
eighteenth-century garb and mount a horse to com-
memorate the Ride of Paul Revere, and a man with a
Swedish name is the author of the most popular biography of Abraham Lincoln. To be American is not, as
the Pole Adam Gurowski pointed out more than a
hundred years ago, a matter of blood; it is a matter of
an idea—and history is the image of that idea.

No, simply piety and blood connection do not account for the appeal, and certainly not for the fact that
the popular interest has been steadily rising, and rising
for nearly twenty years before the natural stir about the

approaching centennial. We can remember that during World War II, the Civil War, not the Revolution, was characteristically used in our propaganda, and that it was the image of Lincoln, not that of Washington or Jefferson, that flashed ritualistically on the silver screen after the double feature; and in classrooms for young Air Force specialists (and perhaps elsewhere), it was sometimes pointed out that the Founding Fathers were not really "democratic," that democracy stemmed from the Civil War.

The turning to the Civil War is, however, a more significant matter than the manipulations of propaganda specialists, and their sometimes unhistorical history. When a people enters upon a period of crisis it is only natural that they look back upon their past and try to find therein some clue to their nature and their destiny—as the kingdom of Judah looked back to the Mosaic period when King Josiah, ensnared in the imperialistic struggles of Egypt, Assyria, and Babylon, instituted the Deuteronomic Reformation, or as the

English, under Elizabeth I, first undertook the study of their own origins and the origins of their church.

World War II merely initiated the period of crisis through which we are passing, and it is only natural that the Civil War looms larger now than ever before. There was a time when the custody of the War was for the most part relegated to the Southerners, but now things are different. We can see this quite simply from the enormous number and sale of books on the War and from the dense population at the Civil War Round Tables.

IN ANY CASE, the War grows in our consciousness. The event stands there larger than life, massively symbolic in its inexhaustible and sibylline significance. Significances, rather, for it is an image of life, and as such is a condensation of many kinds of meanings. There is no one single meaning appropriate to our occasion, and that portentous richness is one of the things that make us stare at the towering event.

We shall not be able to anatomize this portentous richness, but we feel that we must try. We must try because it is a way of understanding our own deeper selves, and that need to understand ourselves is what takes us, always, to the deeper contemplations of art, literature, religion, and history.

To begin with, the Civil War offers a gallery of great human images for our contemplation. It affords a dazzling array of figures, noble in proportion yet human, caught out of Time as in a frieze, in stances so profoundly touching or powerfully mythic that they move us in a way no mere consideration of "historical importance" ever could. We can think of Lincoln alone at night in the drafty corridors of the White House, the shawl on his shoulders; of Jackson's dying words; of Lee coming out of the McLean farmhouse at Appomattox to stare over the heads of his waiting men who crowded around, and strike his gauntleted hands deliberately together; of Sam Davis, with the rope around his neck, giving the Federal soldiers the order for his own execution, the order which General Dodge was too overcome by emotion to give; of Colonel Robert Gould Shaw, Harvard '60, who led his black Fifty-fourth Massachusetts in its first test of manhood, died with the cry, "Forward, my boys!" and was buried under the heaps of his own men in the ditch before Fort Wagner; of Grant, old, discredited, dying of cancer, driving pen over paper, day after day, to tell his truth and satisfy his creditors. That was our Homeric period, and the figures loom up only a little less than gods, but even so, we recognize the lineaments and passions of men, and by that recognition of common kinship share in their grandeur.

Their appeal, and that of their war, is, however, deeper than that. Perhaps we can best understand this by asking why the Civil War appeals so much more strongly to the imagination than does the Revolution. We can start our answer by saying that the Revolution is too simple. That is, it comes to our imagination as white against black, good against bad. It is comfortable, of course, to think that way of the Revolution, even if somewhat unhistorical; but it is not very interesting. It lacks inner drama. We never think, for instance, of Washington or Jefferson caught in dark inner conflicts such as those Lincoln or Lee or Stonewall Jackson experienced. If Washington brooded in the night at Valley Forge, his trouble was not of that order.

But the Civil War—despite Southern nationalism and despite the Southern preference for the "War Between the States"—was, after all, a civil war. And a civil war is, we may say, the prototype of all war, for in the persons of fellow citizens who happen to be the enemy we meet again, with the old ambivalence of love and hate and with all the old guilts, the blood brothers of our childhood. In a civil war—especially in one such as this when the nation shares deep and significant convictions and is not a mere handbasket of factions huddled arbitrarily together by historical happen-so—

all the self-divisions of conflicts within individuals become a series of mirrors in which the plight of the country is reflected, and the self-division of the country a great mirror in which the individual may see imaged his own deep conflicts, not only the conflicts of political loyalties, but those more profoundly personal.

But to return to the contrast between the Revolution and the Civil War, it even seems that something had happened to the American character between 1776 and 1861. Perhaps the historians are right who say that if we look at the portraits of the Founding Fathers we see the faces of men strong, practical, intelligent, and self-assured—and not burdened with excessive sensitivity. But we know that the strength of a Lincoln or a Grant was a different kind of strength, a strength somehow earned out of inner turmoil. Lee was, in a sense, more of an eighteenth-century character than any of them; but from the time of his great decision in 1861, when he said that he would "sacrifice anything but honor" for the Union, to the grim nights when, an old man, he walked the floor of the president's house at Washington College, he appears to us as a man living in the midst of moral scruples arbitrated by an iron will and endured by Christian faith.

The "inwardness" of the experience of the Civil War, in both personal and national terms, made for human sympathy that might without blurring issues, overarch them, and might temper the bigotry of victory and the rancor of defeat. More than one historian has wondered how much the "nervous breakdown" of Lincoln, and the state of soul indicated by his ever-present but controlled melancholy, had to do with his great compassion—and the Gettysburg Address. We may remember how well Grant knew how narrow is the margin between being lost and being saved, and wonder how much the fact that, only two years earlier, he had had to be locked howling drunk in a steamboat cabin, contributed to the dignity and magnanimity of the morning at Appomattox.

We may remember General Simon Bolivar Buckner,

CSA, calling on Grant in his last days of suffering—the same Buckner who had been a classmate at West Point, who had lent Grant money long ago when, destitute and out of the Army, he had come to New York, and who later had surrendered to Grant at Fort Donelson; and remember how, when Buckner had come out from the dying man and the reporters demanded what had passed between them, he said, with tears in his eyes, that it was "too sacred." We may remember the Confederate generals, in their gray sashes, walking as pallbearers at the funeral of Grant.

Then, to round out the picture, we may remember the words of Charles Francis Adams, who had done his share of the fighting, but who said of Lee that had he been in his place he would have done exactly the same. "It may have been treason . . ." he said, "but he awaits sentence at the bar of history in a very respectable company . . ." including John Hampden, Oliver Cromwell, Sir Henry Vane, and George Washington, "a Virginian of note."

The whole context of Southern life made for some sort of self-division. The old romantic unionism survived in the South, and had, as we have said, a pervasive influence. Even in 1860 Virginia's vote for Bell for President, against Breckenridge, indicated the strength of Union sentiment. But more significant than unionism as a source of self-division was the universalist conception of freedom based on natural law, inherited from the Revolution. In addition to the notion of freedom, there were Jacksonian democracy and Christian doctrine, and more than one slaveholder is on record as sympathizing with the distress of a certain Gustavus Henry, who admitted to his wife that "I sometimes think my feelings unfit me for a slaveholder."

The eminent Southern editor Duff Green wrote, in the *United States Telegraph:* "It is only by alarming the consciences of the weak and feeble and diffusing among our people a morbid sensibility on the question of slavery, that the Abolitionists can accomplish their object." The editor, in other words, recognized in his fellow-

Southerners a dangerous proneness to bad conscience and morbid sensibility, ready to be tapped. The greatest danger to slavery was, in one perspective, the Southern heart. Long back, John Randolph of Roanoke, who was no starry-eyed reformer, when asked who was the greatest orator he had ever heard, replied: "A slave, sir. She was a mother and her rostrum was the auction block." And even Calhoun, who as early as 1837 had risen in the Senate to declare slavery not a necessary evil but a positive good, and who was the chief draftsman of the blueprint for Southern society, privately condemned the domestic slave trade.

The philosophy of slavery was shot through with what Louis Hartz calls "agonies and contradictions"—agonies and contradictions clearly exemplified in the fact that the very Constitution of the Confederacy, in forbidding the slave trade, implied that slavery itself was an evil. Behind the formidable façade of logic and learning human beings struggled with the actual process of life. When the Confederate shouldered his musket and marched away, he carried something of this burden. It would not make him falter, for, as General Beauregard said, political and philosophical considerations dwindled when Federal troops set foot on the soil of Virginia, just as such considerations dwindled, for millions in the North, when the first gun was fired at the flag over Sumter.

But for the Confederate the rub was, indeed, real. It was as real as the inner rub we find in documents like this letter written home by a Yankee corporal at Savannah, Georgia, in 1864: "The cruelties practiced on this campaign towards citizens have been enough to blast a more sacred cause than ours. We hardly deserve success."

The inwardness of the story of those characters from the Civil War gives the attraction of drama. In the struggle to define clear aims and certain commitments in the complexity of life, in the struggle to achieve identity and human charity, we find the echo of our own lives, and that fact draws our imagination. We are smuggled into the scene and endure the action.

Here, however, a paradox enters. The similarity to us of those men, the named and nameless, attracts us. But their differences attract us, too.

For we must remember that those men, from conflict and division, rose to strength. From complication they made the simple cutting edge of action. They were, in the deepest sense, individuals; that is, by moral awareness they had achieved, in varying degrees, identity. In our age of conformity, of "other-directedness," of uniformity and the gray flannel suit, of personality created by a charm school, Dale Carnegie, or the public relations expert, when few exhibit "that manly candor and masculine independence of opinion" the dwindling of which de Tocqueville could already deplore before the Civil War—how nostalgically, how romantically, we look back on those powerful and suggestive images of integrity.

As a corollary to our secret yearning for the old-fashioned concept of the person, we may glance, for a moment, at the notion of community. For one thing, the mere sense of place, of a locality clustered about by shared sentiments, looms large in the Civil War. The regimental designations were more than conveniences. Boys marched off from home together and stayed together. Some sense of community went with them. Today, we can scarcely imagine a commander saying what Pickett said to his men as they dressed lines for the fatal charge: "Don't forget today that you are from Old Virginia!" It is absurd—and romantic. But it carries the nostalgic appeal; for the notion of place has a natural relation to the notion of identity in community, in the shared place.

Ultimately, it is the same appeal, even more romantic, which we feel when the old words *duty* and *honor* are spoken by those men. No doubt then many a rogue laid tongue to the words, and no doubt now many a man acts in duty and honor without using the words; but the words speak to us across time of a world of joyfully recognized obligations to the self and to society, and for some even to God.

In our world of restless mobility, where every Main Street looks like the one before and the throughway is always the same, of communication without communion, of the ad-man's nauseating surrogate for family sense and community in the word *togetherness,* we look back nostalgically on the romantic image of some right and natural relation of man to place and man to man, fulfilled in worthy action. The corrosive of historical realism cannot quite disenthrall us of this, nor can our hope that somehow in our modern world we may achieve our own new version, humanly acceptable, of identity and community. In fact, the old image may feed our new hope.

BEYOND NOSTALGIA, and the criticism of ourselves which the nostalgia implies, the Civil War catches the imagination because it raises in an acute and dramatic form a fundamental question, the question of will and inevitability. Back in 1858 William H. Seward, one of the "extreme men" whom Lincoln, the "moderate," was to defeat for the nomination of 1860, had called the struggle between the North and South the "irrepressible conflict," and for generations, historian after historian has asked whether this conflict, arising, as Allan Nevins has said, in a situation of "political drift, cowardice, and fanaticism," and ending in blood, was really irrepressible. Could intelligence, tact, will and good will have averted the arbitrament of force? Was there no solution short of the resolution by blood? Or if the ultimate collision had been averted at that time, would this have meant a mere postponement with more brutal consequences compounded for the future? Or if the conflict became inevitable at a certain date, what was that date—when did the ever-narrowing circle make men so desperate that they had to break out at any cost?

Here we are dealing, of course, with the question of historical inevitability, and the historians do not agree. We find, for example, James G. Randall calling the men of the 1850's the "Blundering Generation." And we find Arthur Schlesinger, Jr., retorting that a society like the South "closed in the defense of evil institutions thus creates moral differences far too profound to be solved by compromise." Or we can turn to Charles A. Beard and find not the moral determinism of Schlesinger but the emphasis on economic factors. But Pieter Geyl, writing on the Civil War, says that the general question of inevitability "is one on which the historian can never form any but an ambivalent opinion. He will now stress other possibilities, then again speak in terms of a coherent sequence of cause and effect. But if he is wise, he will in both cases remain conscious that he has not been able to establish a definite equilibrium between the factors, dissimilar and recalcitrant to exact valuation as they are, by which every crisis situation is dominated." Or to go further, we find that David Donald, in a recent biography of Charles Sumner, can say, quoting André Gide, that "it is the part of wisdom to ask not why, but how events happen." And Kenneth Stampp agrees with Vann Woodward that the whole question "is one for the metaphysician and not the historian."

Strictly speaking, the question of evitability or inevitability is one for the metaphysician, but historians are human, and as human beings they turn, under the shock of event, to consider the "might have been," the road not taken. And as human beings, the historians do not arrive at their conclusions in a vacuum. The speculations of each period arise, of course, in the climate of that period. The history written in the last period of the 19th century, with its emphasis on reconciliation in the new nationalism, is very different from that written in the 1930's under the shadow of Karl Marx. Or more to our present concern, the history written in the 1920's, in a revulsion from war, with aspiration toward a rational internationalism, and with faith in progress, tended to see the Civil War as avoidable—the consequence of strong emotions and weak thinking. And in contrast with this view, we find the historians of our grim period of the Cold War rebuking the implicit optimism of the "revisionists" of the 1920's who held that the Civil War was avoidable.

More than the climate of a period may, however, condition the historian's speculations about inevitability. As human beings, the historians run the risk of letting their view of the objective question of inevitability serve as a mask for gratifying personal need. Southerners, for instance, tend to the view that the Civil War was evitable. And for Southerners this view may serve as a device to share the guilt—just as emphasis on racism in the North may make the Southerner feel a little less lonely in his guilt about slavery. If the War could have been avoided, it is an easy step, then, to show how both sides participated in the responsibility, how the guilt can be spread around. The Southerner may feel that he is stuck with *some* guilt. But he would certainly enjoy the inestimable privilege of being able to call the kettle black. So the evitability theory, though philosophically contradicting the determinism implicit in the Great Alibi, works to the same happy end, the diminishing of guilt.

Northerners, from different motives at different periods, tend to favor the view that the Civil War was inevitable. In one perspective, for some members of earlier generations, living under the bruising and bloody shock of the event, one appeal of the inevitability theory may have been that it relieved the Northerner of certain unpleasant speculations about his own hand in the proceedings. In another perspective, with the inevitability theory there was full justification for the gesture of reconciliation: the Southerner had merely enacted his inevitable role, and might even be congratulated on having enacted it well, for we are all shriven by History. In another perspective, and in another temper, the inevitability theory could be used with equal ease to re-allocate all guilt to the South. The guilt of the South might be taken primarily as a failure to understand the national destiny, or the laws of economics, or the logic of technology, and the virtue of the North would, then, lie in identifying itself with whatever the Wave of the Future might be taken to be. Or the guilt of the South might be put into moral terms: the evil of the South made the Civil War *morally* inevitable, and the North was merely the bright surgical instrument in the hand of God, or History. There is one feature that most versions of the inevitability theory share—any of them may be invoked to demonstrate the blamelessness of the instrument in the hand of the surgeon. So the inevitability theory may work to the same happy end as the Treasury of Virtue.

The Great Alibi and the Treasury of Virtue—they come back again to us as soon as we begin to speculate about the inevitability of the Civil War and undertake the sorting out of causes which that entails. This does not mean that historians should give up the topic. It merely means that historians, and readers of history too, should look twice at themselves when the topic is mentioned. It means that we should seek to end the obscene gratifications of history, and try to learn what the contemplation of the past, conducted with psychological depth and humane breadth, can do for us. What happens if, by the act of historical imagination—the historian's and our own—we are transported into the documented, re-created moment of the past and, in a double vision, see the problems and values of that moment and those of our own, set against each other in mutual criticism and clarification? What happens if, in innocence, we can accept this process without trying to justify the present by the past or the past by the present? We might, then, ask the question about inevitability in the only way that is fruitful—in the recognition that there can never be a *yes-or-no* answer, but that the framing of perspectives of causality and context, as rigorously as possible even though provisionally, fulfills our urgent need to try to determine the limits of responsibility in experience.

The asking and the answering are bound to be ambiguous, for experience carries no labels. But there is a discipline of the mind and heart, a discipline both humbling and enlarging, in the imaginative consideration of possibilities in the face of the unique facts of the irrevocable past. The asking and the answering which history provokes may help us to understand, even to frame, the logic of experience to which we shall submit. History cannot give us a program for the future, but it can give us a fuller understanding of ourselves, and of our common humanity, so that we can better face the future.

In any case, the historians, as human beings, are bound to pick the scab of our fate. They are bound to turn to the question underlying the assessment of all experience: To what extent is man always—or sometimes—trapped in the great texture of causality, of nature and history? Most of us are not metaphysicians

and do not often consider the questions abstractly, but
as men we know that our "felt" answer to it, the answer
in our guts, gives the tone to our living and conditions
the range and vigor of our actions.

The contemplation of the Civil War does not bring
this question to us abstractly. It brings it to us not
only in the very tissue of drama, in the passions of the
actors in the drama, but also as echoed in the drama
we now live and in our own passions. The Civil War
is urgently our war, and, as we have said, reaches in a
thousand ways into our blood stream and our personal
present. But more urgently the present momentous
crisis of our history, when our national existence may
be at stake, makes us demand what we can learn—if,
alas, anything—from that great crisis of our national
past. Does a society like the USSR, "closed in the defense of evil institutions," create "moral differences far
too profound to be solved by compromise"? If so, when
do we start shooting? Or to drop the moral concern,
does the naked geo-political confrontation with Russia

doom us to the struggle? Or the mounting economic rivalry? Can we, in fact, learn only that we are victims of nature and of history? Or can we learn that we can make, or at least have a hand in the making of, our future?

The basic question is anguishing and fascinating, and part of the anguish and fascination is that the question always leads back, past all other problems, to the problems of our personal histories and individual acts. We are living not only in a time of national crisis but in a time of crucial inspection of the nature and role of the individual. And so the Civil War draws us as an oracle, darkly unriddled and portentous, of personal, as well as national, fate.

In any case, the Civil War occurred. "Whether or not the war was inevitable," as Bernard de Voto says, "the crisis was." The conflicts had to be solved, but the fact that "they were not solved short of war is our greatest national tragedy." Or as Sidney Hook has put it: "If the war was inevitable, it was tragic. If it was not inevitable, it was even more tragic."

THE WORD *tragedy* is often used loosely. Here we use it at its deepest significance: the image in action of the deepest questions of man's fate and man's attitude toward his fate. For the Civil War is, massively, that. It is the story of a crime of monstrous inhumanity, into which almost innocently men stumbled; of consequences which could not be trammeled up, and of men who entangled themselves more and more vindictively and desperately until the powers of reason were twisted and their very virtues perverted; of a climax drenched with blood but with nobility gleaming ironically, and redeemingly, through the murk; of a conclusion in which, for the participants at least, there is a reconciliation by human recognition. As Oliver

Wendell Holmes, Jr., said, long before his great fame: "You could not stand up day after day in those indecisive contests where overwhelming victory was impossible because neither side would run as they ought when beaten without getting at least something of the same brotherhood for the enemy that the north pole of a magnet has for the south. . . ."

This is the Southern story, as we read it in the records, have heard it from the lips of old men, or see it in the powerful projections of Faulkner's imagination. But it is more than the Southern story. It is a communal story, as Lincoln said in the Second Inaugural: God gave "to both North and South this terrible war, as the woe due to those by whom the offense came. . . ."

The communal aspect of the story, as Lincoln puts it, means communal guilt as well as communal reconciliation. But in what sense? A writer in the *Journal* of Evansville, Indiana, back in 1861, had taken it that the guilt of the North was in having "winked at the wrongful business" of slavery. Therefore, he said, "the North must not expect to escape the penalty of her lack of principle. She must suffer like the South." Lincoln could scarcely have meant anything that simple; Lincoln had a very clear mind, and the writer of Evansville, Indiana, implies one or the other of two very dubious propositions. First, that if the North had ceased to "wink" there would have been no war; or second, that if there had been a war it would, somehow, have been without suffering.

No, we may hazard that what Lincoln had in mind is a deeper and more complex communal involvement in the event, and in the history of the event, an involvement of all the unworthiness and blunderings of human nature, even of virtues perverted by being abstracted from the proper human context.

From the guilt we turn to the purgation of the Gettysburg Address: "The brave men, living and dead, who struggled here have consecrated it [the cemetery] far above our poor power to add or detract." The soil is hallowed, if Carl Sandburg is right in his reading, by the blood shed communally, the blood of men dying valorously in the common tragic entrapment, and by their valor rising to dignity beyond the entrapment.

Or we can turn to that profoundly revealing moment, shot through with deep ambiguities, when Lincoln, returning by water to Washington from his visit to the fallen Richmond and the headquarters of the victorious army, paused over a passage of the play of Shakespeare which he was reading to his companions. The words he paused to brood over and repeat are, at first glance, peculiar—not words about the ambitious and murderous Macbeth, but words about the good dead victim:

Duncan is in his grave;
After life's fitful fever he sleeps well;
Treason has done his worst; nor steel, nor poison,

Malice domestic, foreign levy, nothing,

Can touch him further.

What comes over to us in this strange moment is no easy applicability, schematically perfect, to the occasion, but rather, the tragic aura of the event. The tone is that of the end of Herman Melville's Supplement to *Battle Pieces,* his poems of the Civil War, issued in 1866: "Let us pray that the terrible historic tragedy of our time may not have been enacted without instructing our whole beloved country through pity and terror. . . ."

Have we been "instructed" by that catharsis of pity and terror?

Sadly, we must answer no. We have not yet achieved justice. We have not yet created a union which is, in the deepest sense, a community. We have not yet resolved our deep dubieties or self-deceptions. In other words, we are sadly human, and in our contemplation of the Civil War we see a dramatization of our humanity; one appeal of the War is that it holds in suspension, beyond all schematic readings and claims to total interpretation, so many of the issues and tragic ironies—somehow essential yet incommensurable—which we yet live.

But there is a deeper appeal. Beyond the satisfaction it may give to rancor, self-righteousness, spite, pride, spiritual pride, vindictiveness, armchair blood lust, and complacency, we can yet see in the Civil War an image of the powerful, painful, grinding process by which an ideal emerges out of history. That should teach us humility beyond the Great Alibi and the Treasury of Virtue, but at the same time it draws us to the glory of the human effort to win meaning from the complex and confused motives of men and the blind ruck of event.

Looking back on the years 1861-65 we see how the individual men, despite failings, blindness, and vice, may affirm for us the possibility of the dignity of life. It is a tragic dignity that their story affirms, but it may evoke strength. And in the contemplation of the story, some of that grandeur, even in the midst of the confused issues, shadowy chances, and brutal ambivalences of our life and historical moment, may rub off on us. And that may be what we yearn for after all.